Meet the
DETROIT
LIONS

By
Zack Burgess

NORWOOD HOUSE PRESS

CHICAGO, ILLINOIS

NORWOOD HOUSE PRESS

P.O. Box 316598 • Chicago, Illinois 60631
For more information about Norwood House Press please visit our website at
www.norwoodhousepress.com or call 866-565-2900.

Photo Credits:
   All photos courtesy of Associated Press, except for the following: National Chicle (6),
   Topps, Inc. (10 both, 11 all, 18), Black Book Archives (15, 23), TCMA, Inc. (22).

   Cover Photo: Peter Read Miller/Associated Press

   The football memorabilia photographed for this book is part of the authors' collection. The collectibles used
   for artistic background purposes in this series were manufactured by many different card companies—
   including Bowman, Donruss, Fleer, Leaf, O-Pee-Chee, Pacific, Panini America, Philadelphia Chewing Gum,
   Pinnacle, Pro Line, Pro Set, Score, Topps, and Upper Deck—as well as several food brands, including
   Crane's, Hostess, Kellogg's, McDonald's and Post.

Designer: Ron Jaffe
Series Editors: Mike Kennedy and Mark Stewart
Project Management: Black Book Partners, LLC.
Editorial Production: Lisa Walsh

LIBRARY OF CONGRESS CATALOGING-IN-PUBLICATION DATA
   Names: Burgess, Zack.
   Title: Meet the Detroit Lions / by Zack Burgess.
   Description: Chicago, Illinois : Norwood House Press, [2016] | Series: Big
      picture sports | Includes bibliographical references and index. |
      Audience: Grade: K to Grade 3.
   Identifiers: LCCN 2015019578| ISBN 9781599537399 (Library Edition : alk.
      paper) | ISBN 9781603578424 (eBook)
   Subjects: LCSH: Detroit Lions (Football team)--Miscellanea--Juvenile
      literature.
   Classification: LCC GV956.D4 B87 2016 | DDC 796.332/640977434--dc23
   LC record available at http://lccn.loc.gov/2015019578

288N—072016
Manufactured in the United States of America in North Mankato, Minnesota

CONTENTS

Words in **bold type** are defined on page 24.

The Lions play tough football.

CALL ME A LION

The lion is known as the king of the jungle. The Detroit Lions work hard to be the kings of the National Football League (NFL). They rely on speed, power, and teamwork. Their fans cheer for them every step of the way. This passion has also helped make Detroit one of America's greatest cities.

TIME MACHINE

The Lions played their first season in Detroit in 1934. Before that, they played in Ohio. The team was called the Spartans. The Lions won the NFL championship three times in the 1950s. Many **Hall of Fame** players have worn Detroit's uniform. **Dutch Clark** and Barry Sanders were two of the best.

"DUTCH" CLARK

Barry Sanders heads for the end zone.

The Lions huddle up at Ford Field.

Best Seat in the House

Michigan gets very cold in the winter. That is why the Lions have played indoors since 1975. In 2002, the team moved to Ford Field in downtown Detroit. It holds 65,000 fans. The stadium is named for the Ford family. They have owned the Lions for more than 50 years.

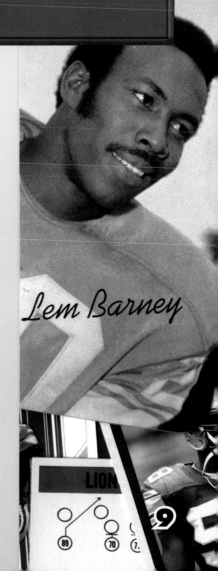

Lem Barney

LION

9

SHOE BOX

The trading cards on these pages show some of the best Lions ever.

BOBBY LAYNE

QUARTERBACK · 1950-1958

Bobby was called the "Blond Bomber" because he loved to throw long passes. He led the Lions to three NFL championships.

JOE SCHMIDT

LINEBACKER · 1953-1965

Joe helped the Lions become one of the NFL's best defensive teams. He knew how to make all of his teammates better.

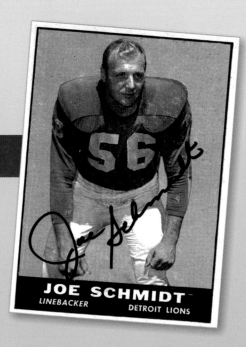

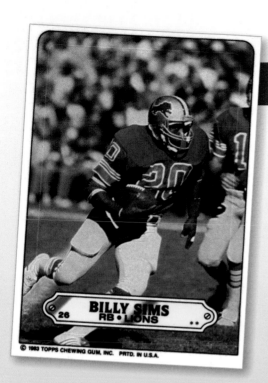

BILLY SIMS

RUNNING BACK · 1980-1984

Billy was the first pick in the 1980 NFL **draft**. He was one of the game's most exciting runners ever.

BARRY SANDERS

RUNNING BACK · 1989-1998

Barry was often the smallest player on the field. His speed and moves made him almost impossible to tackle.

MATTHEW STAFFORD

QUARTERBACK · FIRST YEAR WITH TEAM: 2009

Matthew was a fearless passer. He was just the fourth NFL quarterback to throw for 5,000 yards in a season.

THE BIG PICTURE

Look at the two photos on page 13. Both appear to be the same. But they are not. There are three differences. Can you spot them?

Answers on page 23.

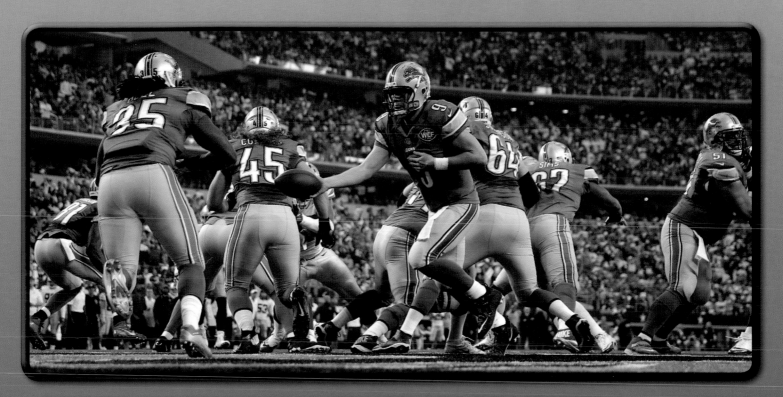

13

TRUE OR FALSE?

Calvin Johnson was a star receiver. Two of these facts about him are **TRUE**. One is **FALSE**. Do you know which is which?

1 Calvin was nicknamed "Megatron" after one of the Transformers.

2 Calvin owns a lion cub named Landry.

3 Calvin set a team record with 1,964 receiving yards in 2012.

Answer on page 23.

Calvin Johnson was one of Detroit's best players ever.

The Lions love to celebrate with their fans.

Go Lions, Go!

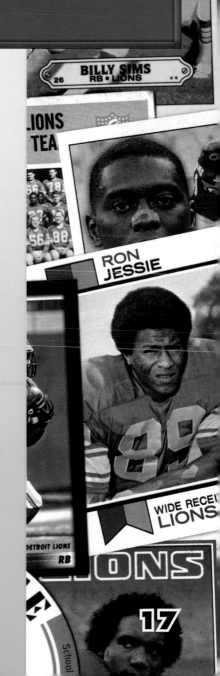

Lions fans wear their team colors with pride. At home, their walls are covered with pennants, posters, and jerseys. At Lions games, fans sing "**Gridiron** Heroes" after every touchdown. They have done this since the 1930s.

ON THE MAP

Here is a look at where five Lions were born, along with a fun fact about each.

 1 JASON HANSON · SPOKANE, WASHINGTON
Jason kicked 495 field goals in 21 seasons for the Lions.

 2 DOAK WALKER · DALLAS, TEXAS
Doak led the NFL in points scored in 1950 and 1955.

 3 LEM BARNEY · GULFPORT, MISSISSIPPI ●————————▶
Lem returned his first NFL **interception** for a touchdown.

 4 HERMAN MOORE · DANVILLE, VIRGINIA
Herman caught more than 100 passes three seasons in a row.

 5 EZEKIEL ANSAH · ACCRA, GHANA
Ezekiel was the team's top pick in the 2013 draft.

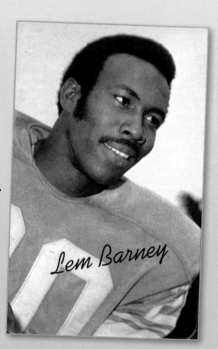

Lem Barney

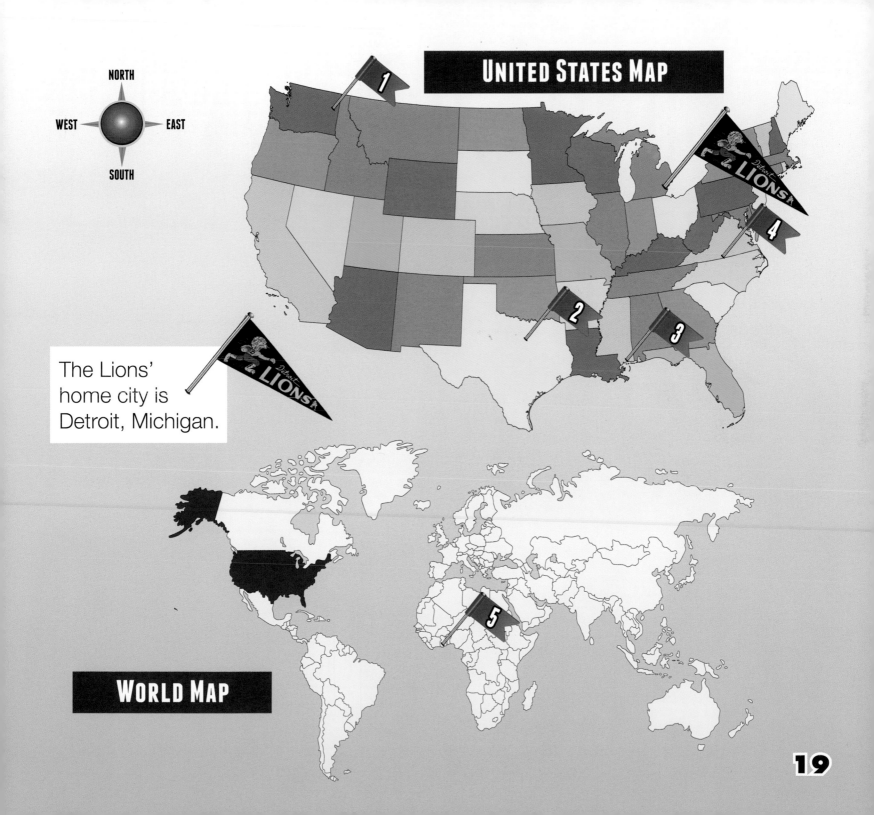

UNITED STATES MAP

The Lions' home city is Detroit, Michigan.

WORLD MAP

19

HOME AND AWAY

DeAndre Levy wears the Lions' home uniform.

Football teams wear different uniforms for home and away games. The Lions' main colors are silver and Honolulu blue. Honolulu is a city in the state of Hawaii.

Golden Tate wears the
Lions' away uniform.

The Lions wear
a silver helmet.
It shows a blue
lion on each side.
The design of
the lion hasn't
changed in more
than 50 years.

WE WON!

The Lions won their first NFL championship in 1935. They were also champs in 1952, 1953, and 1957. The teams of the 1950s had a great offense. But the fans cheered loudest for the defense. Their leaders were Joe Schmidt, Jack Christensen, and **Yale Lary**.

Record Book

These Lions set team records.

Touchdown Passes	Record
Season: Matthew Stafford (2011)	41
Career: Matthew Stafford	163

Touchdown Catches	Record
Season: Calvin Johnson (2011)	16
Career: Calvin Johnson	83

Rushing Yards	Record
Season: **Barry Sanders** (1997)	2,053
Career: Barry Sanders	15,269

Answers for The Big Picture

#45 changed to #55, the football changed to a basketball, and the socks of the player on the far right changed to teal.

Answer for True and False

#2 is false. Calvin does not own a lion cub named Landry.

FOOTBALL WORDS

Draft
The meeting each spring when NFL teams select the top college players.

Gridiron
Another term for football field.

Hall of Fame
The museum in Canton, Ohio, where football's greatest players are honored.

Interception
A pass caught by a defensive player.

INDEX

Photos are on **BOLD** numbered pages.

ABOUT THE AUTHOR

Zack Burgess has been writing about sports for more than 20 years. He has lived all over the country and interviewed lots of All-Pro football players, including Brett Favre, Eddie George, Jerome Bettis, Shannon Sharpe, and Rich Gannon. Zack was the first African American beat writer to cover Major League Baseball when he worked for the *Kansas City Star*.

ABOUT THE LIONS

Learn more at these websites:

www.detroitlions.com • www.profootballhof.com
www.teamspiritextras.com/Overtime/html/lions.html